Letters from under the Banyan Tree

by

Carol Lynn Stevenson Grellas

© 2011, Carol Lynn Stevenson Grellas. All Rights Reserved. This material may not be reproduced in any form, published, reprinted, recorded, performed, broadcast, rewritten or redistributed without explicit permission of Carol Lynn Stevenson Grellas. All such actions are strictly prohibited under law.

Cover art ~ Hadenb

ISBN-13:978-0615685403

Aldrich Press
1840 W 220th Street, Suite 300
Torrance, California 90501

For Jimmy

*We make a dwelling in the evening air,
in which being there together, is enough.*
     – Wallace Stevens

Acknowledgments

Above a Cedar Floor, *Tinfoildresses*
Confessions on your Eleven Days of Dying, *Mad Swirl*
All the Things I Never Read in Poems, *Tryst*
The Unavoidable Crime of Losing Him, *Rusty Truck*
Hearken Back, *Red Ochre*
Letters from Under the Banyan Tree, *Saw Palm Florida Literature and Art*
Upon Finding a Dead Bird in the Garden, *Spoken War Cry*, *Pig 'n a Poke*
Cardiac Arrest, *Foliate Oak*
The Jesus Man, *Foliate Oak*
Exbrook 7/ Your Little Black Book, *Poets & Artists*
An Umbrella Problem, *OVS* (Pushcart nomination)
Broken Player, *Umbrella*
After She's Gone, *Tipton*
Minutes Before, *Medulla*
The Swallow's Begging Call, *Tryst*
Recollections of Summer, *Tinfoildresses*
Inconsolable, *Centrifugal Eye*
Blue Birth, *Contemporary American Voices*
Broken User's Handbook, *Carcinogenic Poetry*
Deliberation After Long Years of Missing Him, *Capers Journal*
Fragments from an Unplanned Mind, *The Stray Branch*
From her Window Veiled in Winter, *Victorian Violet Press* (Pushcart nomination)
Before Waking, *Poets and Artists*

Foreword

Already upon reading the title, Letters from under the Banyan Tree, we become aware of a strong poetic voice that is going to take us somewhere we don't normally go. In these poems of nature and nurture, humans and animals, life and death, Grellas shows us early in her book that the world is not black and white, as learned by a young girl who finds a dead bird: "As if serendipity had placed him along your path . . . so you'd recall both the elation and sorrow of being the one to find him." Grellas then goes on to describe how the bird becomes part of the child. Later, we see again how Grellas blends the natural and the human world, using metaphors of nature to describe a woman's garden while actually describing the woman: "plumped full of juice," "lit from the sun," "draped" and "tartan." The characters in Grellas' poems discover themselves in nature, and she revisits them there often, seeing one of them as "a ghost with flowers" and uniting with another in an alliterative scene: "We became one voice, supple as magnolia leaves falling off a lazy tongue on the blush of beige and whispers." Just as Grellas has lulled us into a nostalgic world of soft white petals, she dives suddenly into the other darker side of nature, "Forgive me, darling, the mushrooms begged me not to but you were so deserving of this wrongdoing," as she poisons her lover. Later she delves completely into the physical aspects of nature with a mathematical poem, "We love to measure the rim of infinity, evaluate the interior of a perfect sphere, the heart inside the whole and the interminable possibilities encompassed within."

In many of the poems, the author walks in liminal space between life and death, "Somewhere between now and yesterday," and she says, "I'm giving you means to unmarked places." At the end
of this fantastical book of what can only be called, "visions," you come to find yourself under the banyan tree, reflecting upon your own flightish dreams and memories which now soar into the bright sun and then dart into the shadows disappearing forever.

Rebecca Moos~ Editor of *Eskimopie.net*

Table of Contents

Upon Finding a Dead Bird in the Garden 10
After She's Gone 13
Minutes Before 15
Broken Player 17
The Swallow's Begging call 19
Exbrook 7/ Your Little Black Book 20
Letters from under the Banyan Tree 21
Hearken Back 22
Above a Cedar Floor 23
An Umbrella Problem 25
Confessions on Your Eleven Days of Dying 26
All the Things I've Never Read in Poems 27
Cry 28
Cardiac Arrest 29
The Jesus Man 30
Recollections of Summer 32
Inconsolable 33
The Unavoidable Crime of Losing Him 34
Blue Birth 35
Deliberation after Long Years of Missing Him 36
Broken User's Handbook 37
Fragments form an Unplanned Mind 38

From her Window Veiled in Winter 39
Before Waking.. 41
About the Author... 42

Upon Finding a Dead Bird in the Garden

When the last moment of a life
was given to you on a green leaf, soaked
with the scent of pink-blush camellias,

where the littlest wings of a resting sparrow
broke half-open against a downy chest,
and feathers spilled over your tiny fingers

soft as sunlight touches a blade of grass
all you could do was cradle that precious flying
thing in the palm of your four-year-old hand;

an open coffin for an eternal viewing, while you
were unknowing death was stealing the breath
of a songbird who'd never sing again…

while you were unaware there was no such thing
as the possibility of another day for the lifeless
memento you'd found on the walk to grandma's

house, before you'd even known for certain
that something could really die. And how you marveled
at that flightless creature you'd imagined willingly

dormant, giving up the gentle push of roving
clouds and his boastful aria through a weightless
sky, all for the pleasure of sleeping, while being held

by you. As if serendipity had placed him along
your path, for a beautiful memory that's haunted
you all these years, so you'd recall both

the elation and sorrow of being the one to find
him, of being the one who touched him last,
of being the one who misunderstood death

as a short pause from living, since anything else
was just too much to bear. How even now
you can almost see him when you close

your eyes. He's become part of your hands,
and in your dreams, you beg him to fly.

After She's Gone

He will remember her orchard, teeming
with cherry tomatoes, plumped full of juice,
like scarlet ornaments lit from the sun
that draped the trellis on long meandering stems,
all but one, fallen beyond the room
of her clapboard house
on a Sunday afternoon.

He will remember her candles, paled
and cold near pieta plaques that lined walls
above old-fashioned wainscot and bleached
wood floors, where she used to sing
and brew Greek coffee from a bottomless
pot that she doesn't pour
on a Sunday afternoon.

He will remember her aged hands
carefully carving the pulpy flesh of vegetables
flushed and sweet; our countless feasts
that she prepared in her tartan tied apron,
this unkempt room, these past due bills,
an empty seat by a windowsill where we'd meet
on a Sunday afternoon.

He will remember her nervous smile,
an unmoving ribcage, the molded outline
in embryo form within the mattress
tattered and worn— a lasting image
that snuck in his being as subtly as incense
or the scent of Livani in the Orthodox
Church while inhaling the sounds during
rounds of the Byzantine Choir
on a Sunday afternoon.

He will remember her kitchen neglected
and bare with a view of overgrown greens
everywhere and a table of knotty pine,
the ripened tomatoes, unpicked and still
on the vine, his sip of ouzo to say goodbye
toasting her name with no reply
on a Sunday afternoon.

Minutes Before

She wanders through the orchard, over
bramble in serpentine steps beneath
the hum of bees, the warm scent of apple

trees permeating greenery where she's
a magpie of memories from another life. Now
she's walking down the aisle, a soon

to be wife, dressed in a brocade gown
her mother standing near with an embellished
handkerchief, holding magnolias

and pearl-braided ribbons, cascading
to the sound of chapel bells. Someone
says *A penny for your thoughts*, inside

her heart's a wishing well, a bank
of forgotten coins. She yells a wordless
scream. Now, she's on a bike, pumping

pedals in a dream, a tattered card between
the spokes flickering through the haze
like a metronome within her mind. The nurse

adjusts her body like a doll devoid of bones
then plumps a pillow for her head,
she can see a rainbow; shades of blue,

the skies are indigo, she hears Clair
de Lune louder than the music of machines
that drone and drip, the children read

a passage from her favorite book.
Now she sees her father rocking in a chair
a pipe between his lips, tobacco

in the air, the nurse says it won't
be long and calls her husband to her side
but she's already gone.

Broken Player

Inside the bellows, behind unmoving keys,
eighty-eight fingers of motionless weight
held her proof of harmony. Her paper-rolls;
a chronicle of life. All songs she once knew.

This was her tomb of inner workings,
her personal sanctum of hushed
melody and muted notes. Once she sang
from the sparkling harp, the curved

body of a walnut case. Once she carried
her music-box memory beside a tracker's
bar, beyond touch, chords and clouds,
beyond the wounds of flesh and saints,

long ago into another life. A place
of arcs in the sky, of light converging
with light. There she moved easily,
barefoot and undressed. There she was fluid

and elegant without words. There her heart
was a pneumatic device that pressed wind
around eternal beings, void of thought
with the echo of hymns. Only the hum

from mouth-less souls through half-lit
moons of apricot stain. Over and over
she yearned for her phantom; a ghost
with flowers that grew deep in the womb

and nourished her ears with a chiming hush.
Sometimes she cleaned the splintering shell
and buffed the cover, tightly closed. A cloth
in her hands, she felt the tremble;

an uncontrolled shake that quaked her
frame. She'd sit at the bench, her hands
crossed neatly for a moment's pause,
allowing herself another birth. So she might

experience that peculiar quiet; that deafening
silence of nothing and nothing. Until all
she heard was the sound of pianos, the voice
of ivory, past lives and bones.

The Swallow's Begging call

I didn't know we forgave each other
until we became one voice, supple
as magnolia leaves falling off a lazy
tongue on the blush of beige and whispers.

I didn't know it was the sound
of her violin but I heard music within
more gorgeous than any harmony ever
aligned in a garden of flowers already opened.

I didn't know I'd witness a miracle
when glass broke to a thousand splintered
parts mirroring the sun's reflection
that echoed every passing face of heaven.

I didn't know her skin would blend
to mine, her tepid body still damp
from the effort of breathing as I felt
her heart move through me, vast
as unconditional love, unbearable
as the silence of leaving…

Exbrook 7/ Your Little Black Book

Here's to the rumpled letters you saved,
the scent of citrus upon your return
when I was almost sleeping, knowing
your love for tangerines after a moonlight
tryst. The stars she gave you, twinkling
through the lining of your coat
as you'd gloat at little gifts unseen but always
there, everything you spoke in French
that made me weep, practiced first
on her, one spared cigarette in a lipstick
case, her face in the mirror overriding my
reflection, the kiln half-open before I heard
you step through the door, a moment
more would have proved a different outcome,
but you were early that night. Forgive me,
darling the mushrooms begged me not
to but you were so deserving
of this wrongdoing and the locket
with her hair took me far beyond the thought
of murder, into Schadenfreude as you
chewed that last spore of poison and I called
her on the phone and said, *come over—
come over and take your things.*

Letters from under the Banyan Tree

When you lie next to me in silence
everything becomes Braille.

There is the bellwether for a place
called hope where a stranger waits

who might know me. I was on
my way to ecstasy, but the tempest

was approaching and reason ruled
the outcome. Needless to say, I never

left my home. Sometimes all you
hold is the end of a tail, and still

you follow thinking there's a body,
just ahead. A note in the bottle is

always visible to creatures in the sea;
letters from under the Banyan Tree.

Hearken Back

I remember my grandmother's hands, her easiness
in life and the way her arms folded over the stillness

of a sleeping heart while resting in a mahogany casket,
as if death was an undying departure; my grandfather's

trumpeted sigh from the other side, too alone to refuse.
I longed to lie down beside her, fingers braided in mine

like the last time she held me before she died until
even her eyes were quiet. I've named my birds after

everyone I've lost and loved. Some days they place
their head inside my hollowed palm and stare with pupils

pinned to mine as I murmur a mourning song proving faith
is never unrequited. And when they fly, old pictures propped

against the wall drift into the other, eliminating all space
between from an unseen waft of air; through the hush of

chaos causing everything to topple; long gone relatives
face to face for the first time in years to the chagrin

of grudges left undone. On the day my mother was buried
I asked that her tombstone be placed at her feet so she might

lie body-length beneath the silence of a Sunlit Oak; limbs
akimbo. But in my dreams she appears wingless and undead

where no goodbye echoes more than leaving or hearkens
back beyond the sound of grieving.

Above a Cedar Floor

You were caged in my closet
for years, because I loved you

to the point of madness. Barred in,
your heart made weak; sweet broken

thing, a tiny sparrow perched
on a wooden branch. Forgive

me. I remember each wing raised
to a sliver of light in-between

my old robe and worn-out raincoat
where half-torn pockets once saved

you from bad weather. Sometimes
I opened the door and listened

as you sang your silent song, barely
audible but loud enough to push

through imaginary clouds in search
of your made-up heaven somewhere

over a rainbow, until the day
I could no longer stand it. The staring

off, far into nothingness as if something
better was just out of reach. So I left

the door knowingly ajar. A sympathetic
moment I cannot explain. One feather

remains in the toggle of my yellow
slicker; a souvenir that lies without

leaving like a small mercy hoping to heal a sin.

An Umbrella Problem

The ubiquitous merit of pi is crucial
for estimating aerial room when ordering
canopies from a nonrefundable source.

Not wanting to remove too much sky
from view could prove tricky had
I not relived sixth grade math every

night with my daughter after evening meals.
So I offered circumference to diameter
ratios and explained irrational numbers;

the value of Euclidean space over calculating
clouds soon obscured from a collapsible shade.
Vinn, the order taker, suggested quadrangles

rather than circles, parallelograms instead
of rounds and rhombuses to curves.
But I told him, we were pi- freaks, my daughter

and I. We love to measure the rim of infinity,
evaluate the interior of a perfect sphere, the heart
inside the whole and the interminable

possibilities encompassed within.

Confessions on Your Eleven Days of Dying

This is for your last days when I pretended
not to know the horror you were living
through every time you pointed your finger

towards the half-light; your knucklebone
trembling with might, like the golden
plover marking its homeward course—

a shearwater navigation of aerodynamic
grace, while I gazed out the window
remembering a place of blue hydrangeas

and singing towers with their unfailing
beauty as if that vision could erase the scene
before me or the broken-hum of gurgling

while I lifted you up for your scheduled dose;
a thimbleful of morphine where no opposing
wind or daughter's selfishness could delay

the hurried wingbeats in your final hours of flying.

All the Things I've Never Read in Poems

The way my blind dog sleeps in the tub;
her porcelain cocoon from twilight till dawn
without water and no lights on.

How two popsicle sticks seemed beautiful the day
they marked the hamster's grave near the swing
set by the magnolia with *save me* scribbled
in purple crayon.

One potpourri heart that hangs from the lamp's
toggle beneath the shade, with a ribbon
made of twine dangling in a golden braid
older than God or so I'm told.

A book of prayers resting in my dresser
drawer with a birthday note, my father's
name inscribed and a tad of doodling
I think he wrote.

The locket in my jewelry box with dimples
left like a raindrop's dented charm from the days
my babies grabbed the chain and cut their teeth
while I held them in my arms.

And the way the scent of opium still lingers
in the air, when I hold my mother's coat,
the one she'd wear everyday stored inside a closet,
somewhere between now and yesterday.

Cry

She was just another organ builder
calculating flow-rate, and velocity,

halving numbers that suited a mother's
kind, but one day her wind-chest filled

with air and I heard a voice like no other
far beyond the bellows, past the doublette

and mechanical keys, where the pedal
board guides the pin, so thin, a fraction

almost too minuscule to report, but the tremor
went deep into my frame; a pneumatic

event surpassing pain like the blow
of breathlessness that makes your knees

buckle into the mahogany cabinet
through the facade and reverberating

case, until it breaks your heart
from rumbling.

Cardiac Arrest

He taught me how to deconstruct
a fraud and told me *phoniness
is not allowed*. Insert a somehow
where the maybes hold a weary

heart to promises. *Don't bend a dying
wish too far.* He said a chest is only winded
when love breathes inside, then leaves
before the cardinal catches air; a flight

as warm as firelight beside the sky.
He was always righter than right
about those kinds of things. I used to watch
him scribble messages on every page;

his diary of daily doings tattooed and dried
in ink; *important chronicles*, he'd say.
Remember you're the history of your life.
His book got buried somewhere deep

beneath a mound of death, but I still
keep a record of his time; unwritten memories
blend with mine that ended without warning—
the way a corn snake kills its prey; suffocation

before the crushing fractures innocent bones.

The Jesus Man

Those were the sweet nights, when summer
came with gladiolus and evenings were made
for riding tandem around our tiny street.
A place were moonbeams bounced off
shingled roofs and angels sang through half
cracked windows, or maybe it was Patty Page—
I've never known for sure.

Somewhere near the dinner hour along
our shady street, a man would stroll in sweat
stained clothes. Most every night we'd see
him come; an enigma with a foolish mind or
maybe it was Jesus Christ—
I've never known for sure.

But how we loved to listen when he mumbled
senseless words. And all the mothers warned
the children, don't befriend that horrid beast,
who had no life, who knew no friend, or maybe
it was all a dream—
I've never known for sure.

I recall one citrine night when chartreuse trees
lined dusk-lit streets, when an oyster moon
slipped down beneath the shadowed boughs
while all the leaves were bright somehow
and we each felt a part of Heaven flicker
or maybe it was just an ache —
I've never known for sure.

We rode our bikes along his path, our fearless
brood; disobeying every rule, defying all
the family laws, until we neared the viaduct,
the place he dubbed his home. Or maybe
it was just a bridge where homeless
people slept on stones—
I've never known for sure.

And though he didn't make a sound
I think we saw him smile at us, in-between
a shooting star, he tapped his knee and almost
grinned as if the Gods were telling us
indifference is a tiny sin,
or maybe unforgivable—
I've never known for sure.

Recollections of Summer

For breakfast we'll lift the birch
boughs and see a deity among
the leaves. Me and you
beneath a veil of sunlight—
a cryptic message like beauty
in the watercress or the way
her casket marked an epiphany
amid opium and lace. I saw Mary's
face when you titled your head
and said, "If we're not careful
we could fall in love again".
But I'm a prisoner quarantined
in dreams where secret prayers
are born. It wasn't easy to save
you. You were Cleopatra, threading
grass sideways between your teeth,
but you never tasted the lightness.
I hear the peacocks cry; their wings
hidden between the magnolias.
It's unnerving here, inside a little
patch of sunshine where this window
makes me think of you and the wind
is just another voice saying goodbye.
Cruel, is the memory of candles
already blown and sitting here
somewhere beside you where my
view has turned to earth.

Inconsolable

Here I lay my tinfoil heart
upon your altar, giver of grace
keeper of angels, maker of life,

taker of days. The dove soars freely
above your lakes, past shallow depths
through hospice clouds and fields

of yellow, threads the summer with
blossoms close, feathered strokes,
wings spread far past wallpaper-weeds,

rusted trees bowed with leaves. And
I am chanting this broken prayer, this
last-chance mantra; oh dreamer

of saints. A sullen lens can pierce
the shadows, find the darkness easy
as light. Lie me down upon the grasses

your birdlime bait; a hunter's
trick. Good rest is needed, my lips
are open. I hear your calling

my spirit flies out, one flutter--
so quick. So quick, so quick.

The Unavoidable Crime of Losing Him

I tried to give him pills, tried to make him normal again—

He was a lone swan on a broken lake, who
wouldn't swim to an unfamiliar place
where the cattails would be too thick for his liking.

*I told him, become what you're meant to be
and nothing will be impossible—*

But he was never sure which was truth or delusion.
He was too soft and I watched him disappear
through clouds until all that was left was
the shadow of an image I could barely see.

*I tried to shock him back to truth, but his
was a better place and nothing could penetrate
that kind of nirvana*

He shot himself under the magnolia tree
down by the lake where the deer lope free.

They say they heard him say *hallelujah*
and I'd like to think someone was listening,
shouted it back, just as his body became

a dispensable but beautiful vessel.

Blue Birth

I'm giving you means to unmarked places.
Where will I go without a yearning?
You'll go towards an inky-world, bruised
blue with madness where bedlam creeps.
But won't I wonder which path to take?
Yes, you'll wonder, but you'll choose a way.
Will it be wrong?
Undeniably wrong.
Well, who will guide me to find my way back?
This is your journey, to find your way back.
But I'll surely fail without halos and wings.
You won't fail.
Will there be halos and wings?
Just look through the bluing of whitened clouds.
And I'll find my way back?
You're already here.

Deliberation after Long Years of Missing Him

A child stands transfixed between
galaxies, eclipsed by light under the soft

corona of stars. An umbilicus is all I know
of him. Where skin has aged like saddened

trees, he was once a part of me. I can't
recall what it was to love him, only

the way his fingers clung to mine
and the slow loosening that followed.

But this is just a dream where he flails
in the far off distance, amid poplars

with three point leaves, where a tourmaline
moon looks like a pregnant mother's

belly, pure as the immaculate conception.

Broken User's Handbook

This was her death by a thousand
cuts, where no prayers could save
how it all began from a broken place

when mercy called her in ill fated
intervals; a dismembering
sentence, one letter at a time.

Where she accepted her destiny
of luckless fool and opened her handbook
to a gardener's cure, when forgiveness

arrived in only one form, when she harvested
poppies that grew beyond the land
of Oz and all things wicked. This was her death

by a thousand cuts, where no prayers
could save her, condemned forever
to a lengthy stab through an empath's

heart till once she grew a dose of opium;
a beatified blur for a hapless life,
but as chance would have it, addiction

prevailed; the coup de grace that healed
each wound from the holiest place
all the way upward through a numbing space—

her pipe still full of petals.

Fragments form an Unplanned Mind

You'll find my slippers beside the fire;
heels worn, rubbed through to sheepskin.
Put them on, come inside this dream.
Here we're swathed by clouds, covered
head to toe in Madonna's hair. No skylights
crowned my mother's casket but I'm sure
she's there, diamonds fixed beneath her tongue
holding Myths and Fables. She tells me
trees are leafed with ribbons like perched
canaries that never fly. I will not forget you.
There is a man who knows the softness
of nipples. He wears his skin inside out,
and worships organs to fractured light. His
sacrifice is all we know of history.

From her Window Veiled in Winter

I'd hold her slippers for ransom but there's no one
left who cares. Even she prefers a barefoot stride

through jasmine. Her perfume is waiting by the dresser.
Sometimes I wear it and imagine she's beside me.

I had to promise to refrain from crying and named
myself an orphan before she died; there was no other way

 to be the nurse of an infant mother. Her perfume
is waiting by the dresser. Evenings were spent lighting

candles.I licked the wicks with prayers. There was always
beauty in the midst of sickness. Flames turned around

and pirouetted like a ballerina on a bottomless floor. Music
cupped her tongue. Evenings were spent lighting candles.

I saw her rising in darkness, everything singed from the fire.
The scent of skin and scorched hair like remnants of a child's

imagination. Daily, she snaps her fingers through clouds,
strumming nails against the moon or wings of flying things.

She prefers a barefoot stride through jasmine. I know because
that sound is unforgettable especially on a windy day. My ears

begin to ache from the reverberation. I put an acorn
in my pocket for good luck. It's a matter of hope, it's a matter

of hope, it's a matter of hope. She blew balloons in the shapes
of clouds and told her children to believe in miracles.

I licked the wicks with prayers, especially on a windy
day. Once she gave me a broken cameo. I can't decide

if it's worth repair. The pin marks are worse than scars.
I remember she wore yellow diamonds. Now she drapes

stars across her breast. There are some things that even
death can't erase. I named myself an orphan before

she died. Come twilight, a white-tailed deer waits
beyond my window. I call out her name, but it's a matter

of hope, and only a fawn squealing for her mother.

Before Waking

He's the stranger you almost know—
his face remembered through a haze
in morning, eyes half-open with a vision

of you in your odalisque-pose
lounging after a midnight tryst;
the scent of skin still lingering

between a braided twist of sheets.
The two of you coupled like a wisteria
tree, your clothes strewn about the room

as if both bodies were ablaze while you
disrobed for the sake of too much
heat, lest the burning grew outside

in, your skin; a silky blend of nudeness
wrapped around him with shadows
married on the wall, until you wake

and there's no-one there at all, it's just
you in an empty room, the light flipped
off by the window's frame, a cocktail

dress slung over a fiddle-back chair,
last night's highball leaked through
a hint of musty air and a dreamed-up

lover without a name.

About the Author

Carol Lynn Stevenson Grellas is a six-time Pushcart nominee and a 2010 Best of the Net nominee. She is the author of seven chapbooks with her latest collection of poems: Epistemology of an Odd Girl, forthcoming from March Street Press. She lives in the High Country, near the base of the Sierra Foothills. According to family lore, she is a direct descendent of Robert Louis Stevenson.

www.ingramcontent.com/pod-product-compliance
Lightning Source LLC
LaVergne TN
LVHW021626080426
835510LV00019B/2780